PORTRAIT OF
SOUTHPORT

ANDY STANSFIELD

HALSGROVE

First published in Great Britain in 2009

Copyright © Andy Stansfield 2009

British Library Cataloguing-in-Publication Data
A CIP record for this title is available from the British Library

ISBN 978 1 84114 874 8

HALSGROVE
Halsgrove House,
Ryelands Industrial Estate,
Bagley Road, Wellington, Somerset TA21 9PZ
Tel: 01823 653777   Fax: 01823 216796
email: sales@halsgrove.com

Part of the Halsgrove group of companies.
Information on all Halsgrove titles is available at: www.halsgrove.com

Printed and bound by Grafiche Flaminia Italy

Previous page: The elegant footbridge crossing the lake in the centre of the seafront gardens.

INTRODUCTION

Southport is typical of many UK seaside resorts in that its main period of development coincided with the reign of Queen Victoria and the coming of the railway. Yet it has a character which is undoubtedly unique. That singularity is given even greater emphasis when examined in the context of its most immediate neighbours along the coast: the port of Liverpool to its south, and to the north boisterous Blackpool, the fishing port of Fleetwood and Morecambe. Each very different indeed.

Unlike its neighbours Southport has evolved with a genteel, sophisticated nature despite a smattering of modern facilities and some which cater solely for younger visitors. The town has long been synonymous with forms of leisure which can only be described as refined: exercising horses along the beach, a leisurely stroll along the pier, window shopping along Lord Street's world famous shopping boulevard or a round of golf on the renowned Royal Birkdale course which attracts thousands of spectators to its major events.

The annual Flower Show, held in Victoria Park, also draws huge crowds from all over the north-west, while the Botanic Gardens Museum is a popular venue which also includes a fine collection of porcelain, local water-colours, plus a section devoted to British birds. Five miles away, at Martin Mere, the Wildfowl and Wetland Trust bird sanctuary provides a haven for hundreds of species of domestic and migratory birds while wildlife enthusiasts can also see red squirrels in the pinewoods of the area, one of a handful of places left in England where our native squirrel survives.

But what I like about the town more than anything, speaking as a photographer, is the way in which scenes continually unfold around you. In any given situation, there is so much visually rich subject matter, so many different angles and viewpoints, without having to move more than a few feet in any direction. It is also possible in many of these instances to imagine the town as it was decades ago. The image on the preceding page is a case in point. Although it appears at first glance to depict a group of happy, chatting nannies from times gone by, it was in fact shot during 2009. My thanks to the ladies concerned and, of course, to their unwitting charges.

But our thanks should really go to a certain William Sutton who in 1798 had the foresight to open the South Port Hotel to cater for the new breed of sea-bathing visitors who were just beginning to discover a select few coastal towns – still too early then to call them resorts. That would follow later. The South Port Hotel was located at was is now the south end of Lord Street, but which was little more than a cluster of fishermen's cottages at the time. Currently the oldest houses along Lord Street, Wellington Terrace, would not be built for another two decades. The Battle of Waterloo would take place during that twenty year interlude.

Other places which find their way into this book were also little more than hamlets in those days: Marshside, Churchtown, Birkdale, Ainsdale. Today they form part of the town as a whole and contain attractive leafy suburbs, often characterised by grand red brick properties which always seem far too large to be family homes.

The collection of images which follows is not intended to be historically comprehensive. Southport has far too many fascinating nooks and crannies for that. Rather, the intention was to capture the essential atmosphere of the town. It is up to you to decide whether or not I have succeeded.

Andy Stansfield

Southport Pier at low tide.

Town centre gardens and Lord Street through the arches of Southport Arts Centre.

6

Shaded walkways.
One side of Lord Street is generously equipped with benches on which to rest in the shade.

Vanishing point.
The pier seems to go for ever, much like the sea at low tide as it disappears out into Morecambe Bay.

Architectural jumble.
Looking back towards the town centre from the beginning of the pier.

Dentist's delight.
There's enough sugar here to fund several dentist practices for years to come.

Ghost ride.
Pleasureland is always a welcome diversion for children.

Colour clash.
The gaudy exterior of Pleasureland is certainly eye-catching and not what might be expected of genteel Southport.

Royal view.
Queen Victoria surveys her empire: a joke
shop and Leo's Bar.

The Hoghton Arms.
Formerly O'Neil's Pub, this town centre inn has had a complete makeover with a traditional exterior but pastel shades inside, making it a popular venue for a drink or a meal.

Shops galore.
Southport's extremely popular pedestrianised shopping precinct, a stone's throw from the railway station.

Local produce.
The rich, almost black till to be found inland from Southport is a market gardener's dream.

Say it with roses.
An elegant display at Southport Flower Show.

Steel band and steel grey skies.
Clouds gather as a steel band entertains the crowd surrounding Victoria Park bandstand with West Indian music.

Dreamer.
This youngster is enthralled by the chequered walkway beside the Town Gardens Café, oblivious even to her chocolate ice cream.

Light and shade.
The War Memorial and elegant wall which surrounds it on one side.

Breather.
A couple take a break from shopping, dwarfed by the pillars of the War Memorial.

This page and opposite: Marine Lake.
The broad footbridge, its paintwork beginning to look weary, which crosses the lake between the Promenade and Marine Drive.

Showpiece.
This gleaming Harley Davidson is propped up on show while its owner, presumably, makes the most of traditional seafront fare for lunch.

Monopoly.
If it's amusement then it must be Silcocks, who seem to own every arcade in town.

Straw hats.
Summer headgear adds to this colourful scene in the town centre while onlookers are being entertained by jazz musicians *(opposite)* during the annual International Jazz Festival.

Summer jazz.
One doesn't normally find deckchairs in the town centre but their bold stripes suit this outdoor jazz event admirably. And what better venue for an outdoor music extravaganza than immediately outside Southport Arts Centre?

Don't miss this.

The Model Railway Village, tucked away behind the Kings Gardens, is a must for young children. Multiple trains are in use at the same time on this huge attractive layout, first opened in 1996 in 1½ acres of sheltered gardens.

A matter of scale.
Reeds and irises reach rooftop height as a colourful freight train approaches the bridge over what is either a tiny stream or a major river.

Lawnmower Museum.
This collection of over 200 exhibits is housed above the Discount Mower Warehouse on Shakespeare Street and makes a fascinating diversion.

All aboard.
Parents and children alike enjoy the Lakeside Miniature Railway which runs through Princes Park alongside the boating lake.

The big W.
The impressive former National &
Provincial Bank, on the corner of Lord
Street and Nevill Street, is now home to
Waterstone's bookshop.

Over the road or over the top?
Never one to be outdone when it comes to street signs and lighting, Southport has excelled itself with this extravagant sign stretching over a small side-street just off the Promenade.

High dive.
One of many sculptures
along the seafront.

38

Downhill racer.
Despite their static nature, the sculptor has imbued a sense of dynamism into each piece of work.

40

Seafront stroll.
This couple are enjoying a late afternoon stroll past the entertainment complex by the
pier.

Opposite: Balustrade and lake.
A walk around the Marine Lake takes in numerous features of interest such as this elegant balustrade.

Royal Birkdale.
The clubhouse of this world-famous golf course nestling among the sand dunes.

Round house.
This unusual property overlooks Royal Birkdale from Waterloo Road.

Churchtown Conservation Area.
Designated in 1974, the Conservation Area protects the Ancient Township of North Meols. This thatched cottage stands by the top of Sally's Lane.

Church Cottage, North Meols.
The porch of Church Cottage, on St Cuthbert's Road, which lies adjacent to St Cuthbert's Parish Church.

Wishful thinking.
This fascinating ivy-clad house, with its strange mixture of architectural features, stands on Saunders Street. Its turret would be an ideal choice for the author's study, providing extensive views of Morecambe Bay as a diversion from work.

Queen Victoria.
The Southport of today is
very much based on
development during the
reign of Queen Victoria, a
fact readily acknowledged
and celebrated by the
town as with this statue
of her in Nevill Street.

Silhouette.
The town centre gardens and Lord Street,
viewed through one of the arches fronting
Southport Arts Centre.

Wader watching.
A foreign visitor takes a closer peek at some of the wading birds on the sands while enjoying his stroll along the pier.

Opposite: Pier and shelter.
The pier stretches out above the extensive sandy beach of Morecambe Bay.

Ornate shelter.
This brightly coloured shelter, with its pagoda-like roof, is one of several built in the same style around the boating lake.

Marine Way Bridge.
An unusual view of the Marine Way Bridge from beneath the section of pier which extends inland across the gardens and boating lake.

Art or architecture?
Marine Way Bridge and the sculpture which marks its beginning.

Opposite: Splash World, Southport's all-weather leisure pool and recreation centre.

Crossing warden.
This natural sculpture was found in the Civic Gardens in Churchtown. Others have been created in a similar vein in the Botanic Gardens too.

Still life.
This elegant arrangement was one of many superb still life displays inside the marquee at Southport Flower Show.

The long walk home.
Southport Pier is 3,650ft long. It had been extended to 4,380ft during 1868 but fire damage reduced it to its present size.

Upright citizens.
Viewed from just above the entertainment complex by the pier, the seafront is a complex pattern of upright features.

Dunes.

The wild landscape to the south of the town is dominated by sand dunes and sharp-edged grasses, honed by the ever-present wind off the sea.

Kite surfing.
Ainsdale Beach is immensely popular with families, kite surfers and even for exercising horses (Red Rum used to train here).

Southport Flower Show.
Tens of thousands of visitors flock to Victoria Park each year for this popular event. Marquees house a wide range of exhibits from local horticultural societies *(above)* to bonsai specialists *(opposite)*.

Pinaceae
"JAPANESE
1946—Info

Chamaecyparis Obtusa
"HINOKI CYPRESS"
1952 – Semi Cascade

63

Martin Mere.
This White-cheeked Pintail, native to the West Indies and south Florida, is seen here at the Wildfowl and Wetlands Trust centre, a short drive from Southport.

Martin Mere.
This charging Emperor Goose is normally more at home in Alaska and is a species which is starting to be under threat of extinction. The WWT perform a vital task in safeguarding Martin Mere's wetland oasis for both indigenous and migratory species.

RSPB hide.
Once a week volunteer Peter Coles mans the RSPB's Sandgrounders' Hide at Marshside
Nature Reserve, an easy walk northwards from the pier.

Tidal flats.
At low tide the mud flats between Marshside and Blackpool in the distance provide a valuable feeding ground for waders.

Ripples.
Strong side-lighting highlights the ripples left in the sand as the tide goes out and the sun sinks in the west.

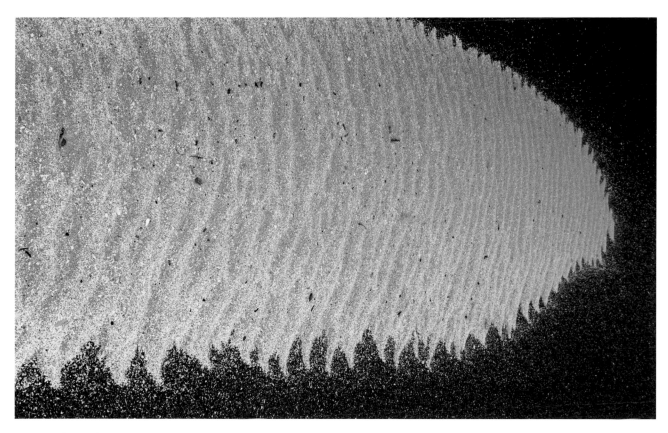

Windblown sand.
Almost resembling a fish, sand has blown up onto the pavement along Marine Drive and has taken on this delicate shape.

We'll keep the red flag flying high…
Not words of the song from the faithful at Old Trafford, but a strongly worded message from the lifeguards that bathing is not permitted at this time.

Victoria Park.
The park's bandstand is an elaborate construction standing proudly aloof in the centre of acres of grass, but several times a year it serves its original purpose for special events.

Lord Street's arcades.
Just one of this famous shopping street's features, the Royal Arcade stands at the southern end of the thoroughfare near to the old railway station.

Cambridge Walks.
Less well known than its counterparts on
the other side of the street, Cambridge
Arcade connects Lord Street with Chapel
Street. It isn't particularly inspiring, in
truth, but Cambridge Walks branches off
from the arcade and is a real delight.

Town Hall.
Completed in 1853 and looking for all the world more like a foreign embassy, the Town Hall's imposing entrance looks out over Lord Street and the town centre gardens.

Preston Bank.
The single storey and windowless Preston Bank was built in 1889 on the west side of Lord Street and is now owned by another bank, HSBC. The triangular pediment is supported by Corinthian columns of polished granite.

Scarisbrick Hotel.
Wherever you are along Lord Street this famous hotel, with the Union flag flying proudly above it, seems to dominate proceedings almost as much as the municipal buildings opposite it.

Classical touch.
These ornate columns are indicative of the degree of care and thought which went into redesigning the town centre's gardens.

Cool.
This fountain becomes a focal point for relaxation on a blisteringly hot day. Note the variety of Lord Street's architectural styles in the background.

Opposite: Graphics.
The redesigned town centre gardens incorporate lots of graphic design, even underfoot.

Botanic Gardens.
This couple enjoy a quiet stroll through
an avenue of mature trees in the Botanic
Gardens.

The range of shapes and colours presented by the trees in the Botanic Gardens is at its best in early autumn.

Botanic Gardens.
Moored beneath overhanging trees, this pleasure boat with its exotic but rather rickety canopy presents a shot of bold colour.

Churchtown.
This elegant lamp standard is one of many which illuminate the streets of Churchtown.

The alternative.
A pier empty of pedestrians, as trippers use the tram instead.

Opposite: Constitutional.
A brisk walk along the pier is *de rigeur* for many of Southport's residents and it can indeed be a rigorous form of exercise on a windy day.

London Square.
Built in 1923 to honour the fallen of the First World War, the War Memorial consists of a central obelisk, seen through a Doric colonnade which is repeated on the far side of the 20m high obelisk in the centre.

London Street.
On each corner of London Square sits an imposing building, each different in style. This one, in Renaissance style, is the National Westminster Bank.

Victoria Park.
Once a year Victoria Park becomes
the temporary home to some exotic
and unusual displays during the
annual Southport Flower Show.

88

North Gardens.
At the northern end of Lord Street, these gardens have recently been redesigned and now include a Nautilus fountain with the theme being carried through with new seating.

Canopies.
Lord Street is renowned for several features, not least its succession of shop front canopies. The full frontage of the Jaeger building (see opposite) can also be seen here.

Opposite: Jaeger building.
Visitors cannot fail to miss the coloured brickwork of the Jaeger shop on Lord Street, towards its northern end.

Park and ride.
To reduce town centre traffic and ease pressure on its car parks, Southport operates an excellent value Park and Ride scheme. Visitors are charged just £1 per day to park here at the Eco Centre, with their car park ticket also serving as a bus ticket for travel into and back out of the town centre.

Opposite: Eco Centre.
Fascinating wall displays explain to visitors some of the easiest ways to conserve energy.

Contemporary architecture.
The new theatre, doubling as a convention centre, is just one of many new buildings which present a bright modern image to Southport's visitors.

Opposite: These pyramids decorate the roof of Morrisons's petrol station.

Leafy suburbs.
Southport's residential areas are just as fascinating to drive around as the town centre. Most areas consist of wide tree-lined roads, which often have large and interesting houses hidden behind the screen of trees.

Lancashire brickwork.
The majority of residences tend to be constructed using Accrington brick, which has a very hard-wearing smooth face and is a distinctive shade of red.

Ornate lamp standard.
I can't remember visiting any
other single location with so
many different styles of
attractive street lighting.

Claim to fame.
Morecambe Bay is renowned for its shrimps.

Storm indicator.
The roof and weather vane on top of an ornate pillar on the seafront, donated to the town by John Fernley in 1861. It also has a drinking fountain, thermometer and barometer.

Lord Street Station.
The elegant clock tower of the old railway station on Lord Street, a line from which used to run through the sand dunes to Chester.

LORD STREET TOWN TRAIL
LORD STREET
STATION
THIS TOWER, BUILT IN 1894, WAS THE ENTRANCE
PORTICO AND CLOCK TOWER TO THE SOUTHPORT
AND CHESHIRE LINES EXTENSION RAILWAY
TERMINUS. THE RAILWAY LINE RAN THROUGH
THE SAND DUNES TO CHESTER.
SOUTHPORT CIVIC SOCIETY

North Meols Civic Gardens.
With St Cuthbert's Parish Church in the
background, this small but lovingly
tended garden serves the community
of Churchtown.

Where there are now borders and a rockery, there used to be an orchard belonging to Sally's Farm. You can still see Sally's Lane and Sally's Cottage just around the corner.

Churchtown.
The Bold Arms Hotel (left) and Hesketh Arms in the background.

Opposite: St Cuthbert's Parish Church and the triangular village green.

Churchtown.
The oldest remaining cottages are characterised by tiny windows and low doors, with several retaining their thatched roofs.

Opposite: The Chocolate Shop tempts passers by with its wares.

109

London Square.
Virtually all the elements of London Square's War Memorial are visible: the obelisk, both colonnades and one of the two reflective pools.

Timepiece.
The clock tower of the Atkinson Art Gallery and Library, which previously served as the Victoria School of Science and Art.

Kings Gardens.
These attractive walkways and flower beds lie between the Promenade and the boating lake.

Seaview.
The Royal Clifton Hotel occupies an extensive stretch of real estate on the east side of the Promenade, overlooking extensive gardens and Morecambe Bay.

Local bye-laws.
A sign forbidding dogs on the beach might be anticipated, but one doesn't expect see a speed limit sign.

Opposite: Moody light over Ainsdale Beach.
In the distance is the silhouetted Lennox oil and natural gas platform. It is actually unmanned and controlled remotely from the Douglas Platform.

Southport Arts Centre.
This lovely stained glass
window can be found on the
first floor of the Arts Centre
which lies between the Town
Hall and the Atkinson Art
Gallery and Library.

116

On the wagon.
The Temperance Institute on London Street,
opposite the railway station.

The Lakeside Inn.
Situated on the Promenade, half way along the Marine Lake, this marks the furthest north of what might be termed town centre facilities for visitors.

Red brick spendour.
Opposite The Lakeside Inn, this splendid red brick building used to be a convalescent hospital.

Rooms with a view.
The former convalescent hospital has now been converted into prestigious apartments.

Opposite: Around the corner, the entrance still indicates the building's original purpose.

Chapel Street.
Temporarily brightened by this balloon seller, the pedestrianised shopping centre is as important for retail businesses as Lord Street.

Mecca bingo hall.
This art deco construction was formerly the Garrick Theatre, opened in 1932, having been built to replace the fire-damaged Opera House on the same site.

Pub quiz question.
Whereabouts in Southport can this cameo of north Africa be found?

Casablanca.
The gaudy former restaurant and bar adjacent
to Pleasureland now lies empty.

Outside the old restaurant, this sign advertises crazy golf with a difference.

Botanic Gardens.
This sculpture is one of a number created from natural materials.

Steps strewn with autumn leaves make an attractive pattern.

Bandstand detail.
Scattered around the town are some wonderful architectural details. This roof detail is from the bandstand in Victoria Park.

Driven to distraction.
Many of the town's roundabouts benefit from some interesting and unusual decoration. This one, at the southern end of the seafront, is sponsored by Mere Brow Smithy.

Simple grandeur.
Often passed, and less frequently noticed, by pedestrians on the east side of Lord Street is the frontage of number 156, The Cottage, one of a row of Regency houses just north of Hill Street.

Wellington Terrace.
At the opposite end of Lord Street, also on the east side, lies this delightful Regency terrace built in 1816-1818 and which constitutes the oldest buildings along Lord Street. The terrace was named after the Duke of Wellington who had been victorious at the Battle of Waterloo in 1815.

Royal visit remembered.
Built at the height of Southport's Victorian expansion, the impressive Prince of Wales Hotel is hidden from casual view by substantial trees and was named after a visit to the town by Prince Edward, the future King Edward VII.

The Bold Hotel.
Built around 1830 as the Bold Arms, while Southport was nothing more than a small village, this is one of the town's oldest hotels.

Sunset over Morecambe Bay.
The glow of the sinking sun is reflected by the timbers and tram rails of the pier.

Pier lighting.
At dusk the lights come on, leading the eye to the amusement arcade and café at the end of the pier.

137

Café culture.
The tree-lined boulevard of Lord Street is an ideal setting for the recent resurgence of coffee bars.

Opposite: Lord Street.
It is often assumed that boulevards were originally a French design, but Southport was equally responsible for developing the idea.

Pier view.
Visitors, wrapped up
against a stiff Spring
breeze off the sea, admire
the view from the end of
the pier.

140

Promenade.
The entire seafront is given visual variety by a diverse collection of sculptures – something to look at when the tide is out, perhaps?

This cycle path runs the length of the seafront.

141

Strike a light.
Even during the daytime, the town's lighting provides a source of striking images.

Flying fish.
At the southern end of the seafront can be found this shoal of fish which rotate as weather vanes.

The End.
Readers who are familiar with my books will know that I like to end on a personal note, with an image which sums up the subject matter of each volume. The three themes in this shot do just that: there is a need to raise one's eyes upwards to fully appreciate Southport's visual fullness; lighting is a vital part of its architecture; and, finally, while the town is very much a visual feast, its history is visible in every corner.